ACCOUNTING

LEDGER BOOK

NAME: ______________________________

PHONE: ____________________________

Accounting Ledger

Year: ______________________ **Sheet Number:** ______________________

No.	Date	Account	Description	Payment (Debit)	Deposit (Credit)	Balance
1.						
2.						
3.						
4.						
5.						
6.						
7.						
8.						
9.						
10.						
11.						
12.						
13.						
14.						
15.						
16.						
17.						
18.						
19.						
20.						
21.						
22.						
23.						
24.						
25.						
26.						
27.						
28.						
29.						
30.						

Accounting Ledger

ar: ____________________ **Sheet Number:** ____________________

.	Date	Account	Description	Payment (Debit)	Deposit (Credit)	Balance

Accounting Ledger

Year: ______________________ **Sheet Number:** ______________________

No.	Date	Account	Description	Payment (Debit)	Deposit (Credit)	Balance
1.						
2.						
3.						
4.						
5.						
6.						
7.						
8.						
9.						
10.						
11.						
12.						
13.						
14.						
15.						
16.						
17.						
18.						
19.						
20.						
21.						
22.						
23.						
24.						
25.						
26.						
27.						
28.						
29.						
30.						

Accounting Ledger

ear: ______________________ **Sheet Number:** ______________________

o.	Date	Account	Description	Payment (Debit)	Deposit (Credit)	Balance
.						
.						
.						
.						
.						
.						
.						
.						
.						
0.						
.						
2.						
3.						
4.						
5.						
6.						
7.						
8.						
9.						
0.						
.						
2.						
3.						
4.						
5.						
6.						
7.						
8.						
9.						
0.						

Accounting Ledger

Year: ______________________ **Sheet Number:** ______________________

No.	Date	Account	Description	Payment (Debit)	Deposit (Credit)	Balance
1.						
2.						
3.						
4.						
5.						
6.						
7.						
8.						
9.						
10.						
11.						
12.						
13.						
14.						
15.						
16.						
17.						
18.						
19.						
20.						
21.						
22.						
23.						
24.						
25.						
26.						
27.						
28.						
29.						
30.						

Accounting Ledger

ear: ______________________ **Sheet Number:** ______________________

o.	Date	Account	Description	Payment (Debit)	Deposit (Credit)	Balance
.						
.						
.						
.						
.						
.						
.						
.						
.						
0.						
1.						
2.						
3.						
4.						
5.						
6.						
7.						
8.						
9.						
0.						
1.						
2.						
3.						
4.						
5.						
6.						
7.						
8.						
9.						
0.						

Accounting Ledger

Year: ______________________ **Sheet Number:** ______________________

No.	Date	Account	Description	Payment (Debit)	Deposit (Credit)	Balance
1.						
2.						
3.						
4.						
5.						
6.						
7.						
8.						
9.						
10.						
11.						
12.						
13.						
14.						
15.						
16.						
17.						
18.						
19.						
20.						
21.						
22.						
23.						
24.						
25.						
26.						
27.						
28.						
29.						
30.						

Accounting Ledger

ear: ______________________ **Sheet Number:** ______________________

.	Date	Account	Description	Payment (Debit)	Deposit (Credit)	Balance

Accounting Ledger

Year: ______________________ **Sheet Number:** ______________________

No.	Date	Account	Description	Payment (Debit)	Deposit (Credit)	Balance
1.						
2.						
3.						
4.						
5.						
6.						
7.						
8.						
9.						
10.						
11.						
12.						
13.						
14.						
15.						
16.						
17.						
18.						
19.						
20.						
21.						
22.						
23.						
24.						
25.						
26.						
27.						
28.						
29.						
30.						

Accounting Ledger

ear: ____________________ **Sheet Number:** ____________________

o.	Date	Account	Description	Payment (Debit)	Deposit (Credit)	Balance

Accounting Ledger

Year: ______________________ **Sheet Number:** ______________________

No.	Date	Account	Description	Payment (Debit)	Deposit (Credit)	Balance
1.						
2.						
3.						
4.						
5.						
6.						
7.						
8.						
9.						
10.						
11.						
12.						
13.						
14.						
15.						
16.						
17.						
18.						
19.						
20.						
21.						
22.						
23.						
24.						
25.						
26.						
27.						
28.						
29.						
30.						

Accounting Ledger

ar: ______________________________ **Sheet Number:** ______________________________

o.	Date	Account	Description	Payment (Debit)	Deposit (Credit)	Balance

Accounting Ledger

Year: ______________________ **Sheet Number:** ______________________

No.	Date	Account	Description	Payment (Debit)	Deposit (Credit)	Balance
1.						
2.						
3.						
4.						
5.						
6.						
7.						
8.						
9.						
10.						
11.						
12.						
13.						
14.						
15.						
16.						
17.						
18.						
19.						
20.						
21.						
22.						
23.						
24.						
25.						
26.						
27.						
28.						
29.						
30.						

Accounting Ledger

ar: ______________________________ **Sheet Number:** ______________________________

	Date	Account	Description	Payment (Debit)	Deposit (Credit)	Balance

Accounting Ledger

Year: ______________________ **Sheet Number:** ______________________

No.	Date	Account	Description	Payment (Debit)	Deposit (Credit)	Balance
1.						
2.						
3.						
4.						
5.						
6.						
7.						
8.						
9.						
10.						
11.						
12.						
13.						
14.						
15.						
16.						
17.						
18.						
19.						
20.						
21.						
22.						
23.						
24.						
25.						
26.						
27.						
28.						
29.						
30.						

Accounting Ledger

Year: ______________________ **Sheet Number:** ______________________

No.	Date	Account	Description	Payment (Debit)	Deposit (Credit)	Balance
1.						
2.						
3.						
4.						
5.						
6.						
7.						
8.						
9.						
10.						
11.						
12.						
13.						
14.						
15.						
16.						
17.						
18.						
19.						
20.						
21.						
22.						
23.						
24.						
25.						
26.						
27.						
28.						
29.						
30.						

Accounting Ledger

Year: ______________________________ **Sheet Number:** ______________________________

No.	Date	Account	Description	Payment (Debit)	Deposit (Credit)	Balance
1.						
2.						
3.						
4.						
5.						
6.						
7.						
8.						
9.						
10.						
11.						
12.						
13.						
14.						
15.						
16.						
17.						
18.						
19.						
20.						
21.						
22.						
23.						
24.						
25.						
26.						
27.						
28.						
29.						
30.						

Accounting Ledger

Year: ______________________ **Sheet Number:** ______________________

No.	Date	Account	Description	Payment (Debit)	Deposit (Credit)	Balance
1.						
2.						
3.						
4.						
5.						
6.						
7.						
8.						
9.						
10.						
11.						
12.						
13.						
14.						
15.						
16.						
17.						
18.						
19.						
20.						
21.						
22.						
23.						
24.						
25.						
26.						
27.						
28.						
29.						
30.						

Accounting Ledger

Year: ______________________ **Sheet Number:** ______________________

No.	Date	Account	Description	Payment (Debit)	Deposit (Credit)	Balance
1.						
2.						
3.						
4.						
5.						
6.						
7.						
8.						
9.						
10.						
11.						
12.						
13.						
14.						
15.						
16.						
17.						
18.						
19.						
20.						
21.						
22.						
23.						
24.						
25.						
26.						
27.						
28.						
29.						
30.						

Accounting Ledger

ear: ______________________ **Sheet Number:** ______________________

o.	Date	Account	Description	Payment (Debit)	Deposit (Credit)	Balance
.						
.						
.						
.						
.						
.						
.						
.						
.						
0.						
1.						
2.						
3.						
4.						
5.						
6.						
7.						
8.						
9.						
0.						
1.						
2.						
3.						
4.						
5.						
6.						
7.						
8.						
9.						
0.						

Accounting Ledger

Year: ______________________ **Sheet Number:** ______________________

No.	Date	Account	Description	Payment (Debit)	Deposit (Credit)	Balance
1.						
2.						
3.						
4.						
5.						
6.						
7.						
8.						
9.						
10.						
11.						
12.						
13.						
14.						
15.						
16.						
17.						
18.						
19.						
20.						
21.						
22.						
23.						
24.						
25.						
26.						
27.						
28.						
29.						
30.						

Accounting Ledger

ear: ______________________ **Sheet Number:** ______________________

o.	Date	Account	Description	Payment (Debit)	Deposit (Credit)	Balance
.						
.						
.						
.						
.						
.						
.						
.						
.						
0.						
1.						
2.						
3.						
4.						
5.						
6.						
7.						
8.						
9.						
0.						
1.						
2.						
3.						
4.						
5.						
6.						
7.						
8.						
9.						
0.						

Accounting Ledger

Year: ______________________ **Sheet Number:** ______________________

No.	Date	Account	Description	Payment (Debit)	Deposit (Credit)	Balance
1.						
2.						
3.						
4.						
5.						
6.						
7.						
8.						
9.						
10.						
11.						
12.						
13.						
14.						
15.						
16.						
17.						
18.						
19.						
20.						
21.						
22.						
23.						
24.						
25.						
26.						
27.						
28.						
29.						
30.						

Accounting Ledger

ear: ______________________ **Sheet Number:** ______________________

o.	Date	Account	Description	Payment (Debit)	Deposit (Credit)	Balance
.						
.						
.						
.						
.						
.						
.						
.						
.						
).						
..						
2.						
3.						
4.						
5.						
6.						
7.						
8.						
9.						
).						
..						
2.						
3.						
4.						
5.						
6.						
7.						
8.						
9.						
).						

Accounting Ledger

Year: ______________________ **Sheet Number:** ______________________

No.	Date	Account	Description	Payment (Debit)	Deposit (Credit)	Balance
1.						
2.						
3.						
4.						
5.						
6.						
7.						
8.						
9.						
10.						
11.						
12.						
13.						
14.						
15.						
16.						
17.						
18.						
19.						
20.						
21.						
22.						
23.						
24.						
25.						
26.						
27.						
28.						
29.						
30.						

Accounting Ledger

ear: ______________________________ **Sheet Number:** ______________________________

o.	Date	Account	Description	Payment (Debit)	Deposit (Credit)	Balance

Accounting Ledger

Year: ______________________ **Sheet Number:** ______________________

No.	Date	Account	Description	Payment (Debit)	Deposit (Credit)	Balance
1.						
2.						
3.						
4.						
5.						
6.						
7.						
8.						
9.						
10.						
11.						
12.						
13.						
14.						
15.						
16.						
17.						
18.						
19.						
20.						
21.						
22.						
23.						
24.						
25.						
26.						
27.						
28.						
29.						
30.						

Accounting Ledger

ear: ______________________ **Sheet Number:** ______________________

o.	Date	Account	Description	Payment (Debit)	Deposit (Credit)	Balance
.						
.						
.						
.						
.						
.						
.						
.						
.						
0.						
1.						
2.						
3.						
4.						
5.						
6.						
7.						
8.						
9.						
0.						
1.						
2.						
3.						
4.						
5.						
6.						
7.						
8.						
9.						
0.						

Accounting Ledger

Year: ______________________ **Sheet Number:** ______________________

No.	Date	Account	Description	Payment (Debit)	Deposit (Credit)	Balance
1.						
2.						
3.						
4.						
5.						
6.						
7.						
8.						
9.						
10.						
11.						
12.						
13.						
14.						
15.						
16.						
17.						
18.						
19.						
20.						
21.						
22.						
23.						
24.						
25.						
26.						
27.						
28.						
29.						
30.						

Accounting Ledger

ar: ______________________ **Sheet Number:** ______________________

o.	Date	Account	Description	Payment (Debit)	Deposit (Credit)	Balance

Accounting Ledger

Year: ______________________ **Sheet Number:** ______________________

No.	Date	Account	Description	Payment (Debit)	Deposit (Credit)	Balance
1.						
2.						
3.						
4.						
5.						
6.						
7.						
8.						
9.						
10.						
11.						
12.						
13.						
14.						
15.						
16.						
17.						
18.						
19.						
20.						
21.						
22.						
23.						
24.						
25.						
26.						
27.						
28.						
29.						
30.						

Accounting Ledger

ear: ______________________ **Sheet Number:** ______________________

o.	Date	Account	Description	Payment (Debit)	Deposit (Credit)	Balance
.						
.						
.						
.						
.						
.						
.						
.						
.						
0.						
1.						
2.						
3.						
4.						
5.						
6.						
7.						
8.						
9.						
0.						
1.						
2.						
3.						
4.						
5.						
6.						
7.						
8.						
9.						
0.						

Accounting Ledger

Year: ______________________________ **Sheet Number:** ______________________________

No.	Date	Account	Description	Payment (Debit)	Deposit (Credit)	Balance
1.						
2.						
3.						
4.						
5.						
6.						
7.						
8.						
9.						
10.						
11.						
12.						
13.						
14.						
15.						
16.						
17.						
18.						
19.						
20.						
21.						
22.						
23.						
24.						
25.						
26.						
27.						
28.						
29.						
30.						

Accounting Ledger

ear: ______________________ **Sheet Number:** ______________________

o.	Date	Account	Description	Payment (Debit)	Deposit (Credit)	Balance
.						
.						
.						
.						
.						
.						
.						
.						
.						
0.						
1.						
2.						
3.						
4.						
5.						
6.						
7.						
8.						
9.						
0.						
1.						
2.						
3.						
4.						
5.						
6.						
7.						
8.						
9.						
0.						

Accounting Ledger

Year: ______________________

Sheet Number: ______________________

No.	Date	Account	Description	Payment (Debit)	Deposit (Credit)	Balance
1.						
2.						
3.						
4.						
5.						
6.						
7.						
8.						
9.						
10.						
11.						
12.						
13.						
14.						
15.						
16.						
17.						
18.						
19.						
20.						
21.						
22.						
23.						
24.						
25.						
26.						
27.						
28.						
29.						
30.						

Accounting Ledger

ear: ______________________ **Sheet Number:** ______________________

o.	Date	Account	Description	Payment (Debit)	Deposit (Credit)	Balance
.						
.						
.						
.						
.						
.						
.						
.						
.						
0.						
1.						
2.						
3.						
4.						
5.						
6.						
7.						
8.						
9.						
0.						
1.						
2.						
3.						
4.						
5.						
6.						
7.						
8.						
9.						
0.						

Accounting Ledger

Year: ______________________________ **Sheet Number:** ______________________________

No.	Date	Account	Description	Payment (Debit)	Deposit (Credit)	Balance
1.						
2.						
3.						
4.						
5.						
6.						
7.						
8.						
9.						
10.						
11.						
12.						
13.						
14.						
15.						
16.						
17.						
18.						
19.						
20.						
21.						
22.						
23.						
24.						
25.						
26.						
27.						
28.						
29.						
30.						

Accounting Ledger

ear: ______________________ **Sheet Number:** ______________________

o.	Date	Account	Description	Payment (Debit)	Deposit (Credit)	Balance
.						
.						
.						
.						
.						
.						
.						
.						
.						
0.						
1.						
2.						
3.						
4.						
5.						
6.						
7.						
8.						
9.						
0.						
1.						
2.						
3.						
4.						
5.						
6.						
7.						
8.						
9.						
0.						

Accounting Ledger

Year: ______________________ **Sheet Number:** ______________________

No.	Date	Account	Description	Payment (Debit)	Deposit (Credit)	Balance
1.						
2.						
3.						
4.						
5.						
6.						
7.						
8.						
9.						
10.						
11.						
12.						
13.						
14.						
15.						
16.						
17.						
18.						
19.						
20.						
21.						
22.						
23.						
24.						
25.						
26.						
27.						
28.						
29.						
30.						

Accounting Ledger

ear: ______________________ **Sheet Number:** ______________________

o.	Date	Account	Description	Payment (Debit)	Deposit (Credit)	Balance

Accounting Ledger

Year: ______________________ **Sheet Number:** ______________________

No.	Date	Account	Description	Payment (Debit)	Deposit (Credit)	Balance
1.						
2.						
3.						
4.						
5.						
6.						
7.						
8.						
9.						
10.						
11.						
12.						
13.						
14.						
15.						
16.						
17.						
18.						
19.						
20.						
21.						
22.						
23.						
24.						
25.						
26.						
27.						
28.						
29.						
30.						

Accounting Ledger

ear: ______________________ **Sheet Number:** ______________________

.	Date	Account	Description	Payment (Debit)	Deposit (Credit)	Balance

Accounting Ledger

Year: ______________________ **Sheet Number:** ______________________

No.	Date	Account	Description	Payment (Debit)	Deposit (Credit)	Balance
1.						
2.						
3.						
4.						
5.						
6.						
7.						
8.						
9.						
10.						
11.						
12.						
13.						
14.						
15.						
16.						
17.						
18.						
19.						
20.						
21.						
22.						
23.						
24.						
25.						
26.						
27.						
28.						
29.						
30.						

Accounting Ledger

ear: ______________________________ **Sheet Number:** ______________________________

.	Date	Account	Description	Payment (Debit)	Deposit (Credit)	Balance

Accounting Ledger

Year: ______________________ **Sheet Number:** ______________________

No.	Date	Account	Description	Payment (Debit)	Deposit (Credit)	Balance
1.						
2.						
3.						
4.						
5.						
6.						
7.						
8.						
9.						
10.						
11.						
12.						
13.						
14.						
15.						
16.						
17.						
18.						
19.						
20.						
21.						
22.						
23.						
24.						
25.						
26.						
27.						
28.						
29.						
30.						

Accounting Ledger

ear: ____________________ **Sheet Number:** ____________________

o.	Date	Account	Description	Payment (Debit)	Deposit (Credit)	Balance
.						
.						
.						
.						
.						
.						
.						
.						
.						
0.						
.						
2.						
3.						
4.						
5.						
6.						
7.						
8.						
9.						
0.						
.						
2.						
3.						
4.						
5.						
6.						
7.						
8.						
9.						
0.						

Accounting Ledger

Year: ______________________ **Sheet Number:** ______________________

No.	Date	Account	Description	Payment (Debit)	Deposit (Credit)	Balance
1.						
2.						
3.						
4.						
5.						
6.						
7.						
8.						
9.						
10.						
11.						
12.						
13.						
14.						
15.						
16.						
17.						
18.						
19.						
20.						
21.						
22.						
23.						
24.						
25.						
26.						
27.						
28.						
29.						
30.						

Accounting Ledger

ar: ______________________________ **Sheet Number:** ______________________________

	Date	Account	Description	Payment (Debit)	Deposit (Credit)	Balance

Accounting Ledger

Year: ______________________ **Sheet Number:** ______________________

No.	Date	Account	Description	Payment (Debit)	Deposit (Credit)	Balance
1.						
2.						
3.						
4.						
5.						
6.						
7.						
8.						
9.						
10.						
11.						
12.						
13.						
14.						
15.						
16.						
17.						
18.						
19.						
20.						
21.						
22.						
23.						
24.						
25.						
26.						
27.						
28.						
29.						
30.						

Accounting Ledger

ear: ______________________ **Sheet Number:** ______________________

o.	Date	Account	Description	Payment (Debit)	Deposit (Credit)	Balance
.						
.						
.						
.						
.						
.						
.						
.						
.						
).						
l.						
2.						
3.						
4.						
5.						
5.						
7.						
3.						
9.						
).						
l.						
2.						
3.						
4.						
5.						
5.						
7.						
3.						
9.						
).						

Accounting Ledger

Year: ______________________ **Sheet Number:** ______________________

No.	Date	Account	Description	Payment (Debit)	Deposit (Credit)	Balance
1.						
2.						
3.						
4.						
5.						
6.						
7.						
8.						
9.						
10.						
11.						
12.						
13.						
14.						
15.						
16.						
17.						
18.						
19.						
20.						
21.						
22.						
23.						
24.						
25.						
26.						
27.						
28.						
29.						
30.						

Accounting Ledger

ear: ____________________ **Sheet Number:** ____________________

o.	Date	Account	Description	Payment (Debit)	Deposit (Credit)	Balance

Accounting Ledger

Year: ______________________ **Sheet Number:** ______________________

No.	Date	Account	Description	Payment (Debit)	Deposit (Credit)	Balance
1.						
2.						
3.						
4.						
5.						
6.						
7.						
8.						
9.						
10.						
11.						
12.						
13.						
14.						
15.						
16.						
17.						
18.						
19.						
20.						
21.						
22.						
23.						
24.						
25.						
26.						
27.						
28.						
29.						
30.						

Accounting Ledger

ear: ______________________ **Sheet Number:** ______________________

o.	Date	Account	Description	Payment (Debit)	Deposit (Credit)	Balance
.						
.						
.						
.						
.						
.						
.						
.						
.						
0.						
1.						
2.						
3.						
4.						
5.						
6.						
7.						
8.						
9.						
0.						
1.						
2.						
3.						
4.						
5.						
6.						
7.						
8.						
9.						
0.						

Accounting Ledger

Year: ______________________ **Sheet Number:** ______________________

No.	Date	Account	Description	Payment (Debit)	Deposit (Credit)	Balance
1.						
2.						
3.						
4.						
5.						
6.						
7.						
8.						
9.						
10.						
11.						
12.						
13.						
14.						
15.						
16.						
17.						
18.						
19.						
20.						
21.						
22.						
23.						
24.						
25.						
26.						
27.						
28.						
29.						
30.						

Accounting Ledger

ar: ______________________________ **Sheet Number:** ______________________________

.	Date	Account	Description	Payment (Debit)	Deposit (Credit)	Balance

Accounting Ledger

Year: ______________________ **Sheet Number:** ______________________

No.	Date	Account	Description	Payment (Debit)	Deposit (Credit)	Balance
1.						
2.						
3.						
4.						
5.						
6.						
7.						
8.						
9.						
10.						
11.						
12.						
13.						
14.						
15.						
16.						
17.						
18.						
19.						
20.						
21.						
22.						
23.						
24.						
25.						
26.						
27.						
28.						
29.						
30.						

Accounting Ledger

ar: ______________________ **Sheet Number:** ______________________

.	Date	Account	Description	Payment (Debit)	Deposit (Credit)	Balance

Accounting Ledger

Year: ______________________ **Sheet Number:** ______________________

No.	Date	Account	Description	Payment (Debit)	Deposit (Credit)	Balance
1.						
2.						
3.						
4.						
5.						
6.						
7.						
8.						
9.						
10.						
11.						
12.						
13.						
14.						
15.						
16.						
17.						
18.						
19.						
20.						
21.						
22.						
23.						
24.						
25.						
26.						
27.						
28.						
29.						
30.						

Accounting Ledger

ear: ____________________ **Sheet Number:** ____________________

o.	Date	Account	Description	Payment (Debit)	Deposit (Credit)	Balance

Accounting Ledger

Year: ____________________ **Sheet Number:** ____________________

No.	Date	Account	Description	Payment (Debit)	Deposit (Credit)	Balance
1.						
2.						
3.						
4.						
5.						
6.						
7.						
8.						
9.						
10.						
11.						
12.						
13.						
14.						
15.						
16.						
17.						
18.						
19.						
20.						
21.						
22.						
23.						
24.						
25.						
26.						
27.						
28.						
29.						
30.						

Accounting Ledger

ear: ______________________ **Sheet Number:** ______________________

o.	Date	Account	Description	Payment (Debit)	Deposit (Credit)	Balance

Accounting Ledger

Year: ______________________ **Sheet Number:** ______________________

No.	Date	Account	Description	Payment (Debit)	Deposit (Credit)	Balance
1.						
2.						
3.						
4.						
5.						
6.						
7.						
8.						
9.						
10.						
11.						
12.						
13.						
14.						
15.						
16.						
17.						
18.						
19.						
20.						
21.						
22.						
23.						
24.						
25.						
26.						
27.						
28.						
29.						
30.						

Accounting Ledger

ear: ____________________ **Sheet Number:** ____________________

o.	Date	Account	Description	Payment (Debit)	Deposit (Credit)	Balance
.						
.						
.						
.						
.						
.						
.						
.						
.						
0.						
1.						
2.						
3.						
4.						
5.						
6.						
7.						
8.						
9.						
0.						
1.						
2.						
3.						
4.						
5.						
6.						
7.						
8.						
9.						
0.						

Accounting Ledger

Year: ______________________ **Sheet Number:** ______________________

No.	Date	Account	Description	Payment (Debit)	Deposit (Credit)	Balance
1.						
2.						
3.						
4.						
5.						
6.						
7.						
8.						
9.						
10.						
11.						
12.						
13.						
14.						
15.						
16.						
17.						
18.						
19.						
20.						
21.						
22.						
23.						
24.						
25.						
26.						
27.						
28.						
29.						
30.						

Accounting Ledger

ear: ______________________ **Sheet Number:** ______________________

o.	Date	Account	Description	Payment (Debit)	Deposit (Credit)	Balance

Accounting Ledger

Year: ______________________ **Sheet Number:** ______________________

No.	Date	Account	Description	Payment (Debit)	Deposit (Credit)	Balance
1.						
2.						
3.						
4.						
5.						
6.						
7.						
8.						
9.						
10.						
11.						
12.						
13.						
14.						
15.						
16.						
17.						
18.						
19.						
20.						
21.						
22.						
23.						
24.						
25.						
26.						
27.						
28.						
29.						
30.						

Accounting Ledger

ear: ______________________________ **Sheet Number:** ______________________________

o.	Date	Account	Description	Payment (Debit)	Deposit (Credit)	Balance

Accounting Ledger

Year: ______________________ **Sheet Number:** ______________________

No.	Date	Account	Description	Payment (Debit)	Deposit (Credit)	Balance
1.						
2.						
3.						
4.						
5.						
6.						
7.						
8.						
9.						
10.						
11.						
12.						
13.						
14.						
15.						
16.						
17.						
18.						
19.						
20.						
21.						
22.						
23.						
24.						
25.						
26.						
27.						
28.						
29.						
30.						

Accounting Ledger

ear: ______________________ **Sheet Number:** ______________________

o.	Date	Account	Description	Payment (Debit)	Deposit (Credit)	Balance
.						
.						
.						
.						
.						
.						
.						
.						
.						
.						
.						
.						
.						
.						
.						
.						
.						
.						
.						
.						
.						
.						
.						
.						
.						
.						
.						
.						
.						
.						

Accounting Ledger

Year: ______________________ **Sheet Number:** ______________________

No.	Date	Account	Description	Payment (Debit)	Deposit (Credit)	Balance
1.						
2.						
3.						
4.						
5.						
6.						
7.						
8.						
9.						
10.						
11.						
12.						
13.						
14.						
15.						
16.						
17.						
18.						
19.						
20.						
21.						
22.						
23.						
24.						
25.						
26.						
27.						
28.						
29.						
30.						

Accounting Ledger

ear: ______________________________ **Sheet Number:** ______________________________

o.	Date	Account	Description	Payment (Debit)	Deposit (Credit)	Balance

Accounting Ledger

Year: ______________________ **Sheet Number:** ______________________

No.	Date	Account	Description	Payment (Debit)	Deposit (Credit)	Balance
1.						
2.						
3.						
4.						
5.						
6.						
7.						
8.						
9.						
10.						
11.						
12.						
13.						
14.						
15.						
16.						
17.						
18.						
19.						
20.						
21.						
22.						
23.						
24.						
25.						
26.						
27.						
28.						
29.						
30.						

Accounting Ledger

ear: ____________________ **Sheet Number:** ____________________

o.	Date	Account	Description	Payment (Debit)	Deposit (Credit)	Balance

Accounting Ledger

Year: ______________________ **Sheet Number:** ______________________

No.	Date	Account	Description	Payment (Debit)	Deposit (Credit)	Balance
1.						
2.						
3.						
4.						
5.						
6.						
7.						
8.						
9.						
10.						
11.						
12.						
13.						
14.						
15.						
16.						
17.						
18.						
19.						
20.						
21.						
22.						
23.						
24.						
25.						
26.						
27.						
28.						
29.						
30.						

Accounting Ledger

ear: ______________________ **Sheet Number:** ______________________

o.	Date	Account	Description	Payment (Debit)	Deposit (Credit)	Balance
.						
.						
.						
.						
.						
.						
.						
.						
.						
).						
l.						
2.						
3.						
4.						
5.						
6.						
7.						
8.						
9.						
).						
l.						
2.						
3.						
4.						
5.						
6.						
7.						
8.						
9.						
).						

Accounting Ledger

Year: ______________________ **Sheet Number:** ______________________

No.	Date	Account	Description	Payment (Debit)	Deposit (Credit)	Balance
1.						
2.						
3.						
4.						
5.						
6.						
7.						
8.						
9.						
10.						
11.						
12.						
13.						
14.						
15.						
16.						
17.						
18.						
19.						
20.						
21.						
22.						
23.						
24.						
25.						
26.						
27.						
28.						
29.						
30.						

Accounting Ledger

ear: ____________________ **Sheet Number:** ____________________

o.	Date	Account	Description	Payment (Debit)	Deposit (Credit)	Balance
.						
.						
.						
.						
.						
.						
.						
.						
.						
0.						
1.						
2.						
3.						
4.						
5.						
6.						
7.						
8.						
9.						
0.						
1.						
2.						
3.						
4.						
5.						
6.						
7.						
8.						
9.						
0.						

Accounting Ledger

Year: ____________________ **Sheet Number:** ____________________

No.	Date	Account	Description	Payment (Debit)	Deposit (Credit)	Balance
1.						
2.						
3.						
4.						
5.						
6.						
7.						
8.						
9.						
10.						
11.						
12.						
13.						
14.						
15.						
16.						
17.						
18.						
19.						
20.						
21.						
22.						
23.						
24.						
25.						
26.						
27.						
28.						
29.						
30.						

Accounting Ledger

ear: ______________________ **Sheet Number:** ______________________

o.	Date	Account	Description	Payment (Debit)	Deposit (Credit)	Balance

Accounting Ledger

Year: ______________________ **Sheet Number:** ______________________

No.	Date	Account	Description	Payment (Debit)	Deposit (Credit)	Balance
1.						
2.						
3.						
4.						
5.						
6.						
7.						
8.						
9.						
10.						
11.						
12.						
13.						
14.						
15.						
16.						
17.						
18.						
19.						
20.						
21.						
22.						
23.						
24.						
25.						
26.						
27.						
28.						
29.						
30.						

Accounting Ledger

ar: ______________________ **Sheet Number:** ______________________

.	Date	Account	Description	Payment (Debit)	Deposit (Credit)	Balance

Accounting Ledger

Year: ______________________ **Sheet Number:** ______________________

No.	Date	Account	Description	Payment (Debit)	Deposit (Credit)	Balance
1.						
2.						
3.						
4.						
5.						
6.						
7.						
8.						
9.						
10.						
11.						
12.						
13.						
14.						
15.						
16.						
17.						
18.						
19.						
20.						
21.						
22.						
23.						
24.						
25.						
26.						
27.						
28.						
29.						
30.						

Accounting Ledger

ear: ____________________ **Sheet Number:** ____________________

.	Date	Account	Description	Payment (Debit)	Deposit (Credit)	Balance

Accounting Ledger

Year: ______________________ **Sheet Number:** ______________________

No.	Date	Account	Description	Payment (Debit)	Deposit (Credit)	Balance
1.						
2.						
3.						
4.						
5.						
6.						
7.						
8.						
9.						
10.						
11.						
12.						
13.						
14.						
15.						
16.						
17.						
18.						
19.						
20.						
21.						
22.						
23.						
24.						
25.						
26.						
27.						
28.						
29.						
30.						

Accounting Ledger

ear: ______________________________ **Sheet Number:** ______________________________

.	Date	Account	Description	Payment (Debit)	Deposit (Credit)	Balance

Accounting Ledger

Year: ____________________ **Sheet Number:** ____________________

No.	Date	Account	Description	Payment (Debit)	Deposit (Credit)	Balance
1.						
2.						
3.						
4.						
5.						
6.						
7.						
8.						
9.						
10.						
11.						
12.						
13.						
14.						
15.						
16.						
17.						
18.						
19.						
20.						
21.						
22.						
23.						
24.						
25.						
26.						
27.						
28.						
29.						
30.						

Accounting Ledger

ear: ____________________ **Sheet Number:** ____________________

o.	Date	Account	Description	Payment (Debit)	Deposit (Credit)	Balance

Accounting Ledger

Year: ______________________ **Sheet Number:** ______________________

No.	Date	Account	Description	Payment (Debit)	Deposit (Credit)	Balance
1.						
2.						
3.						
4.						
5.						
6.						
7.						
8.						
9.						
10.						
11.						
12.						
13.						
14.						
15.						
16.						
17.						
18.						
19.						
20.						
21.						
22.						
23.						
24.						
25.						
26.						
27.						
28.						
29.						
30.						

Accounting Ledger

ear: ______________________ **Sheet Number:** ______________________

o.	Date	Account	Description	Payment (Debit)	Deposit (Credit)	Balance
1.						
2.						
3.						
4.						
5.						
6.						
7.						
8.						
9.						
0.						
1.						
2.						
3.						
4.						
5.						
6.						
7.						
8.						
9.						
0.						
1.						
2.						
3.						
4.						
5.						
6.						
.						
.						
.						
.						

Accounting Ledger

Year: ______________________________ **Sheet Number:** ______________________________

No.	Date	Account	Description	Payment (Debit)	Deposit (Credit)	Balance
1.						
2.						
3.						
4.						
5.						
6.						
7.						
8.						
9.						
10.						
11.						
12.						
13.						
14.						
15.						
16.						
17.						
18.						
19.						
20.						
21.						
22.						
23.						
24.						
25.						
26.						
27.						
28.						
29.						
30.						

Accounting Ledger

ear: ______________________________ **Sheet Number:** ______________________________

o.	Date	Account	Description	Payment (Debit)	Deposit (Credit)	Balance

Accounting Ledger

Year: ______________________ **Sheet Number:** ______________________

No.	Date	Account	Description	Payment (Debit)	Deposit (Credit)	Balance
1.						
2.						
3.						
4.						
5.						
6.						
7.						
8.						
9.						
10.						
11.						
12.						
13.						
14.						
15.						
16.						
17.						
18.						
19.						
20.						
21.						
22.						
23.						
24.						
25.						
26.						
27.						
28.						
29.						
30.						

Accounting Ledger

ar: ______________________________ **Sheet Number:** ______________________________

o.	Date	Account	Description	Payment (Debit)	Deposit (Credit)	Balance

Accounting Ledger

Year: ______________________ **Sheet Number:** ______________________

No.	Date	Account	Description	Payment (Debit)	Deposit (Credit)	Balance
1.						
2.						
3.						
4.						
5.						
6.						
7.						
8.						
9.						
10.						
11.						
12.						
13.						
14.						
15.						
16.						
17.						
18.						
19.						
20.						
21.						
22.						
23.						
24.						
25.						
26.						
27.						
28.						
29.						
30.						

Accounting Ledger

ear: ______________________________ **Sheet Number:** ______________________________

.	Date	Account	Description	Payment (Debit)	Deposit (Credit)	Balance
.						
.						
.						
.						
.						
.						
.						
.						
.						
.						
.						
.						
.						
.						
.						
.						
.						
.						
.						
.						
.						

Accounting Ledger

Year: ______________________ **Sheet Number:** ______________________

No.	Date	Account	Description	Payment (Debit)	Deposit (Credit)	Balance
1.						
2.						
3.						
4.						
5.						
6.						
7.						
8.						
9.						
10.						
11.						
12.						
13.						
14.						
15.						
16.						
17.						
18.						
19.						
20.						
21.						
22.						
23.						
24.						
25.						
26.						
27.						
28.						
29.						
30.						

Accounting Ledger

ear: ______________________ **Sheet Number:** ______________________

o.	Date	Account	Description	Payment (Debit)	Deposit (Credit)	Balance

Accounting Ledger

Year: ______________________ **Sheet Number:** ______________________

No.	Date	Account	Description	Payment (Debit)	Deposit (Credit)	Balance
1.						
2.						
3.						
4.						
5.						
6.						
7.						
8.						
9.						
10.						
11.						
12.						
13.						
14.						
15.						
16.						
17.						
18.						
19.						
20.						
21.						
22.						
23.						
24.						
25.						
26.						
27.						
28.						
29.						
30.						

Accounting Ledger

ear: ______________________________ **Sheet Number:** ______________________________

o.	Date	Account	Description	Payment (Debit)	Deposit (Credit)	Balance

Accounting Ledger

Year: ____________________ **Sheet Number:** ____________________

No.	Date	Account	Description	Payment (Debit)	Deposit (Credit)	Balance
1.						
2.						
3.						
4.						
5.						
6.						
7.						
8.						
9.						
10.						
11.						
12.						
13.						
14.						
15.						
16.						
17.						
18.						
19.						
20.						
21.						
22.						
23.						
24.						
25.						
26.						
27.						
28.						
29.						
30.						

Accounting Ledger

ar: ______________________________ **Sheet Number:** ______________________________

.	Date	Account	Description	Payment (Debit)	Deposit (Credit)	Balance

Accounting Ledger

Year: ______________________ **Sheet Number:** ______________________

No.	Date	Account	Description	Payment (Debit)	Deposit (Credit)	Balance
1.						
2.						
3.						
4.						
5.						
6.						
7.						
8.						
9.						
10.						
11.						
12.						
13.						
14.						
15.						
16.						
17.						
18.						
19.						
20.						
21.						
22.						
23.						
24.						
25.						
26.						
27.						
28.						
29.						
30.						

Accounting Ledger

ear: ____________________ **Sheet Number:** ____________________

o.	Date	Account	Description	Payment (Debit)	Deposit (Credit)	Balance

Accounting Ledger

Year: ______________________ **Sheet Number:** ______________________

No.	Date	Account	Description	Payment (Debit)	Deposit (Credit)	Balance
1.						
2.						
3.						
4.						
5.						
6.						
7.						
8.						
9.						
10.						
11.						
12.						
13.						
14.						
15.						
16.						
17.						
18.						
19.						
20.						
21.						
22.						
23.						
24.						
25.						
26.						
27.						
28.						
29.						
30.						

Accounting Ledger

ear: ______________________ **Sheet Number:** ______________________

o.	Date	Account	Description	Payment (Debit)	Deposit (Credit)	Balance

Accounting Ledger

Year: ____________________ **Sheet Number:** ____________________

No.	Date	Account	Description	Payment (Debit)	Deposit (Credit)	Balance
1.						
2.						
3.						
4.						
5.						
6.						
7.						
8.						
9.						
10.						
11.						
12.						
13.						
14.						
15.						
16.						
17.						
18.						
19.						
20.						
21.						
22.						
23.						
24.						
25.						
26.						
27.						
28.						
29.						
30.						

Accounting Ledger

ear: ______________________ **Sheet Number:** ______________________

o.	Date	Account	Description	Payment (Debit)	Deposit (Credit)	Balance

Accounting Ledger

Year: ____________________ **Sheet Number:** ____________________

No.	Date	Account	Description	Payment (Debit)	Deposit (Credit)	Balance
1.						
2.						
3.						
4.						
5.						
6.						
7.						
8.						
9.						
10.						
11.						
12.						
13.						
14.						
15.						
16.						
17.						
18.						
19.						
20.						
21.						
22.						
23.						
24.						
25.						
26.						
27.						
28.						
29.						
30.						

Accounting Ledger

ear: ____________________ **Sheet Number:** ____________________

o.	Date	Account	Description	Payment (Debit)	Deposit (Credit)	Balance

Accounting Ledger

Year: ____________________ **Sheet Number:** ____________________

No.	Date	Account	Description	Payment (Debit)	Deposit (Credit)	Balance
1.						
2.						
3.						
4.						
5.						
6.						
7.						
8.						
9.						
10.						
11.						
12.						
13.						
14.						
15.						
16.						
17.						
18.						
19.						
20.						
21.						
22.						
23.						
24.						
25.						
26.						
27.						
28.						
29.						
30.						

Accounting Ledger

ear: ______________________ **Sheet Number:** ______________________

o.	Date	Account	Description	Payment (Debit)	Deposit (Credit)	Balance

Accounting Ledger

Year: ______________________ **Sheet Number:** ______________________

No.	Date	Account	Description	Payment (Debit)	Deposit (Credit)	Balance
1.						
2.						
3.						
4.						
5.						
6.						
7.						
8.						
9.						
10.						
11.						
12.						
13.						
14.						
15.						
16.						
17.						
18.						
19.						
20.						
21.						
22.						
23.						
24.						
25.						
26.						
27.						
28.						
29.						
30.						

Accounting Ledger

ear: ______________________ **Sheet Number:** ______________________

o.	Date	Account	Description	Payment (Debit)	Deposit (Credit)	Balance

Accounting Ledger

Year: ______________________ **Sheet Number:** ______________________

No.	Date	Account	Description	Payment (Debit)	Deposit (Credit)	Balance
1.						
2.						
3.						
4.						
5.						
6.						
7.						
8.						
9.						
10.						
11.						
12.						
13.						
14.						
15.						
16.						
17.						
18.						
19.						
20.						
21.						
22.						
23.						
24.						
25.						
26.						
27.						
28.						
29.						
30.						

Accounting Ledger

ear: ____________________ **Sheet Number:** ____________________

o.	Date	Account	Description	Payment (Debit)	Deposit (Credit)	Balance
.						
.						
.						
.						
.						
.						
.						
.						
.						
.						
.						
.						
.						
.						
.						
.						
.						
.						
.						
.						
.						
.						
.						
.						
.						
.						
.						
.						
.						
.						

Accounting Ledger

Year: ____________________ **Sheet Number:** ____________________

No.	Date	Account	Description	Payment (Debit)	Deposit (Credit)	Balance
1.						
2.						
3.						
4.						
5.						
6.						
7.						
8.						
9.						
10.						
11.						
12.						
13.						
14.						
15.						
16.						
17.						
18.						
19.						
20.						
21.						
22.						
23.						
24.						
25.						
26.						
27.						
28.						
29.						
30.						

Accounting Ledger

ar: ______________________________ **Sheet Number:** ______________________________

o.	Date	Account	Description	Payment (Debit)	Deposit (Credit)	Balance

Accounting Ledger

Year: ______________________ **Sheet Number:** ______________________

No.	Date	Account	Description	Payment (Debit)	Deposit (Credit)	Balance
1.						
2.						
3.						
4.						
5.						
6.						
7.						
8.						
9.						
10.						
11.						
12.						
13.						
14.						
15.						
16.						
17.						
18.						
19.						
20.						
21.						
22.						
23.						
24.						
25.						
26.						
27.						
28.						
29.						
30.						

CPSIA information can be obtained
at www.ICGtesting.com
Printed in the USA
BVHW051050150221
600147BV00011B/828

9 781964 8063